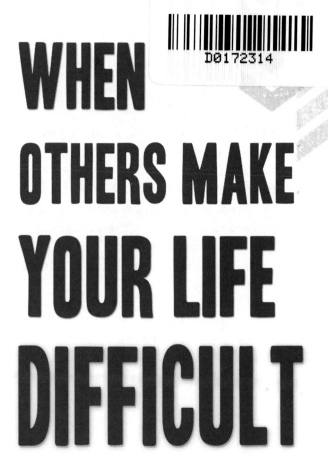

WHEN OTHERS MAKE YOUR LIFE DIFFICULT

ISBN: 978-1-941213-28-5
Text layout design: Sharon Troyer
Cover design: Teresa Sommers
Illustrations: Jerron Hess

Printed in the USA
Fourth printing: October 2015

Published by:
TGS International
PO Box 355
Berlin, OH 44610 USA

TGS001074   www.tgsinternational.com

WHEN OTHERS MAKE YOUR LIFE DIFFICULT

Daniel E. Miller

TABLE OF CONTENTS

INTRODUCTION

We share this earth with fellow humans. Together we drive the streets, walk the trails, and breathe the air. Sometimes this co-existence is peaceful and pleasant. Other times it is not. Close interaction breeds friction. Selfish individuals find their desires in conflict with the desires of others. Unhappy people seem determined to spread their gloom. In ways both large and small, people make life difficult for one another. Indeed, all of us have experienced the trauma of troubled relationships.

We begin this study by thinking about God. It is impossible to properly understand ourselves and others unless we understand the One who created us. As we understand Him and His purpose for us, we can more honestly evaluate our lives. Why do we relate to others the way we do? Why do we cultivate relationships at all? In our relationships, what kinds of behaviors do we find offensive? All of these questions can be answered as we look honestly inward.

Moving beyond ourselves, we must consider the needs and desires of others. When we are affected by their negative behaviors, we can choose to focus on their wrong actions, or we can go deeper, trying to understand the motives, longings, and needs that are driving the behavior.

Sometimes human relationships seem hopeless. Fractures that have persisted for years seem beyond healing. Sarcastic responses, shouting matches, ridicule, and intimidation become habitual. In such relationships, beginning to relate in love seems awkward and humiliating. Our attempts to heal relationships may be rebuffed, making future efforts seem impossible.

However, there *is* hope. The God who "is able to do exceeding abundantly above all that we ask or think" (Eph. 3:20) is a God who wants to heal broken relationships. His purpose for us is to learn His way of love, relying on His strength to live in peace and freedom, even when others make life difficult.

1

UNDERSTANDING GOD

God that made the world and all things therein,
seeing that he is Lord of heaven and earth, dwel-
leth not in temples made with hands.
—Acts 17:24

As a student in high school and college, I remember periodic feelings of mental exhaustion. After trying so hard to grasp the complexities of algebra or the rules of economics, I suddenly came to a place where I felt I couldn't absorb the material. At times it seemed that, in spite of my efforts, my mind just didn't have the capacity to wrap itself around the concepts being taught.

Sometimes we have similar feelings when we think about God. Trying to comprehend the One who has always existed and who will always exist, who created everything and needs nothing, can be challenging for the human mind. As created beings, we can never fully understand the mind of the infallible Being who created us, saved us, and sustains us.

However, this reality must be balanced with the truth that we can know God. In fact, His desire for relationship with us is what motivated Him  to create us (Acts 17:26–27; Revelation 4:11). Just as in human relationships a person changes from a stranger to an acquaintance to an intimate friend, so our relationship with God is designed to progress to ever deeper levels of intimacy and understanding. The good news is that we will never reach a place where we know God as deeply as He can be known; no matter how long we live or how long we have known the Lord, there is always more to learn about Him.

Learning to know God involves understanding the many aspects of His character and how they blend into one perfect whole. Emphasis on His mercy for mankind must be balanced with the truth of His justice that demands repentance from sin. His impeccable holiness must be weighed alongside His forgiveness and grace.

In all this learning, the object is far more than an academic exercise to develop an accurate picture of God; the purpose of this pursuit is to allow the knowledge of Him to shape our earthly lives and prepare us for the heavenly. Without this knowledge, we are destined to go astray. In the words of A.W. Tozer, "It is impossible to keep our moral practices sound and our inward attitudes right while our idea of God is erroneous or inadequate."[1]

On the other hand, the better we learn to know God, the more Christ-like our behavior will become. Standing in awe at the holiness of God will drive us toward holiness. Sensing the immensity of His mercy toward us will motivate us to show compassion. Comprehending His love for the world will open our eyes to the needs of others. Then, as we begin to understand the love in the heart of God, we will realize that He is asking us to extend that love, not only to the lovable, but also to the irritating.

---

1   A.W. Tozer, *The Knowledge of the Holy* (New York: Harper Books, 1961), p. viii.

2

UNDERSTANDING CREATION

I have made the earth, and created man upon it: I, even my hands, have stretched out the heavens, and all their host have I commanded.
—Isaiah 45:12

As humans, we are used to basing our thoughts and opinions on things we have experienced. We are only vaguely aware of things outside our experiential frame of reference. This is how it is when we think about the time before Creation. We can hardly imagine what it must have been like for Almighty God to take a watery, uninhabited sphere and turn it into a magnificent home for people and animals. We can barely conceive of a time when there were no humans, or what it would have been like to be one of only two people on the entire face of the earth. These are things

13

we must accept by faith, understanding "that the worlds were framed by the word of God, so that things which are seen were not made of things which do appear" (Hebrews 11:3).

So why did God create us and give us a world in which to live? What is the purpose for our existence? Colossians 1:16 gives us the answer: it says everything was created for God. That includes things as diverse as sycamore trees and salamanders, Neptune and the Nile River, mangoes and the Milky Way. Most important, it includes us.

We have been created for God! He made us because He wanted us. Revelation 4:11 expands on that concept when it says that we were created for God's pleasure. The thought is revolutionary, breathtaking—almost presumptuous! Why would

a God who crafted planets and stars care about someone as weak and vulnerable as I? Can He really get pleasure from such a struggling mortal?

The answer is yes; He can and He does! Not only does He find pleasure in us, but He created us to find pleasure in Him. By creating us in His image and giving us living souls, He designed us to find deep satisfaction only through a dependent relationship with Him (Genesis 1:27; 2:7).

We are told in Acts 17:28 that in Him we have our being. In other words, we can accurately understand our own identity and place in the world only when we understand our position as beings created by God and for God. And it is only with this understanding that we can truly understand others.

3

UNDERSTANDING MYSELF

O LORD, thou hast searched me, and known me.
Thou knowest my downsitting and mine uprising,
thou understandest my thought afar off.
—Psalm 139:1–2

For a period of time when I was a teenager, almost every Sunday afternoon I was overcome with a feeling of heaviness that snatched away my joy and made me look at the world through gray, depressed lenses. While I could identify several possible reasons for this Sunday afternoon sadness, there was something mysterious about it. I did not really know why I felt the way I did.

Probably all of us can remember times like this, times when we have been unable to say why we feel the way we do. We don't understand ourselves!

In times like these, it is comforting to remember

that our Creator does understand us, and He wants to help us understand ourselves. Just as we call up the manufacturer of our electronic gadgets when we don't understand how to make them work, so God invites us to ask Him when we don't understand how we, His creation, think and function.

Hearing from God through prayer and time in His Word will help us in the journey to understanding ourselves. Receiving the input and observations of our friends and family is also valuable. As we listen to God and others and analyze our own actions and reactions, certain truths will emerge.

We noted earlier that God created us for Himself, and that in doing so, He created us to need Him. Our emotional needs were designed by Him to draw us to Him. However, sin has complicated that design. Sin takes our God-given longings and twists them into self-serving manipulation. It blinds us to the source of true satisfaction and convinces us that we will be happy if we pursue counterfeits. Notice some ways we often allow our longings to lead us into destructive behaviors:

- We want to be loved, so we try to live up to the expectations of others.
- We want to be noticed, so we engage in attention-getting behavior.
- We want to be valued, so we try to devalue those around us.
- We want to be needed, so we try to impress others with how indispensable we are.
- We want to be safe, so we try to eradicate anything that might harm us.

Sadly, these strategies will not work. Trying to satisfy our longings in these ways only makes us even more emotionally empty. Tragically, we often are not aware of the inner longings that cause these behaviors. In our constant efforts to fill the emptiness of our souls, we fail to stop and analyze what is driving us.

In fact, this is the condition of every soul that does not know Christ and has not accepted His provision. A verse from the song, "Rescue the Perishing," says it well:

> Down in the human heart, crushed by the tempter,
> Feelings lie buried that grace can restore.
> Touched by a loving heart, awakened by kindness,
> Chords that were broken will vibrate once more.[1]

As believers, we have been awakened to the reality that God wants a relationship with us—wants it so much that He bought us back when we were serving the enemy. This assurance of His amazing love gives us a foundation of security on which our emotions can rest.

This does not mean life will be easy. People may malign and threaten us. They may try to make us feel worthless and insecure. These things can devastate us unless we have firmly established

---

1   Fanny Crosby (song in public domain).

ourselves in Christ. Resting in His unchanging goodness gives us a security that allows us to reach out to others with understanding and love.

4

SPIRITUAL DEVELOPMENT— THE JOURNEY

Now no chastening for the present seemeth to be joyous, but grievous: nevertheless afterward it yieldeth the peaceable fruit of righteousness unto them which are exercised thereby.
—Hebrews 12:11

Longing filled me this morning. It is February, season of the almond blossoms. For most of the past three years, I lived in the Holy Land, and every spring I savored their beauty. This year, I am not there. The almond trees are blooming without me.

The almond blossoms are not only beautiful but also symbolic. Winter in Palestine is dreary, damp, and chilly. The barren, rocky landscape stretches in unbroken monotony. Then, suddenly, sprigs of tender pink and white foliage appear, gladdening the world. The almond trees are blooming.

Sometimes my life faces winter. People don't understand me; no one really seems to care about what I am going through. I feel rejected and alone in the world.

Contrary to some popular teaching, the life of the believer is not a continual carefree existence. When we choose to follow the teachings of Jesus, we invite difficulty. Think of Jesus' words: "If any man will come after me, let him deny himself, and take up his cross daily, and follow me" (Luke 9:23). A cross is an object of suffering, shame, and difficulty. While Jesus was not suggesting that we pick up literal wooden crosses, He was acknowledging that following Him involves that same reproach. Not only do His teachings and His example of servanthood run counter to our natural inclinations, but they also invite the scorn and rejection of others, perhaps even family members and friends. This, too, was anticipated by Jesus. He said, "Think not that I am come to send peace on earth: I came not to send peace, but a sword. . . . And a man's foes shall be they of his own household" (Matthew 10:34, 36).

What does this look like practically? How does bearing the cross affect our daily lives? What are the ways we may be called to suffer?

The answers will be different for every individual. Maybe your neighbor will drive across your lawn on a muddy day, leaving big ruts. Maybe your co-worker will blame his mistake on you, and you will lose your job. Maybe your sibling will influence your parents to reduce your share of the inheritance. Depending where you live, you may be jailed for your faith.

Sometimes in the middle of this suffering, we despair. Although we know we have been called to suffer for the cause of Christ, the suffering we are experiencing seems too intense for anyone to bear.

What we often forget in times like these is that this suffering has a deeper purpose. It is producing character in us. It is preparing us for days of joy ahead. This is why James said, "My brethren, count it all joy when ye fall into divers temptations; knowing this, that the trying of your faith worketh patience" (James 1:2–3).

This is what it means to walk with Christ. Experiencing the beauty of His likeness in our lives demands spiritual development—and spiritual development requires suffering. There are no shortcuts or substitutes. The way of Christ is the way of the cross.

And yet we have the promise of the almond blossoms. After dismal days, joy will break through. After seasons of suffering, we will emerge to find ourselves purified. New desires, fresh courage, and renewed vision will propel us as we continue the journey from earth to heaven.

5

UNDERSTANDING OTHERS

For who maketh thee to differ from another? and
what hast thou that thou didst not receive?
—1 Corinthians 4:7a

A crowded terminal in an international airport is a microcosm of the world, and I love the cultural perspectives it provides. As I sit at the gate waiting to board the plane, the conservative Middle Eastern family, the chattering Hispanic youngsters, and the staid European couple all reinforce or challenge my preconceived ideas. If I'm sitting close enough and can understand the language, I even get to listen in on conversations and catch brief glimpses of how total strangers perceive reality.

While these times of observation remind us of the tremendous diversity in our world, they also

reveal another, almost contradictory truth: people are amazingly similar.

Whether we live in a Bedouin tent or a Manhattan penthouse, we need love, acceptance, and security. We need other people. We want to express ourselves. We want to know and be known. We are the same.

And yet we are different. The God whose creative word birthed both deserts and rain forests is the same God who delighted in diversity when He created people. We come into the world not only with physical differences but also with different talents and temperaments. Furthermore, from conception onward, we are shaped by our unique environments—our families, our communities, our culture, our education, and our finances.

When we observe the actions of others, our human tendency is to assume that their motives are the same as ours would have been had we engaged in that behavior. However, this assumption is a flawed premise for understanding others. A person's motives are influenced by both personality and background, and similar actions can easily spring from very different motives.

So why do we assume sameness? Why do we so quickly interpret another's behavior through our own defaults? It is because, in many ways, we *are* so similar. We all mourn death, avoid pain, dread disease, and protect self-interests. We all like good food, comfortable clothes, understanding friends, and beautiful sunsets.

It is precisely this seeming contradiction—that we are at the same time incredibly similar and incredibly different—that creates tension in human relationships. We are offended when others do not mean to offend, and we offend others when we do not mean to. We fail to understand how differently others think from how we think; they fail to see how similar our desires are to theirs.

Learning to understand others is a key to overcoming the difficulties they bring into our lives.

Consider the person who offended. What are the ongoing circumstances this person is dealing with? What are the factors in his or her background that might cause this behavior? Most important, how can we have a positive influence on him or her?

When we approach conflicts with a genuine desire to really understand others, we are well on the way to solving those conflicts.

6

CONFLICT

For what glory is it, if, when ye be buffeted for your faults, ye shall take it patiently? but if, when ye do well, and suffer for it, ye take it patiently, this is acceptable with God.
—1 Peter 2:20

As I write this, the nation of Syria is engaged in a civil war. Iran and Israel are waging a clandestine battle with nuclear implications. Countries like Lebanon, Turkey, Ukraine, and South Sudan are rife with internal conflicts. And every day in the Unites States, hundreds of marriages end in divorce.

We live in a world of conflict. Conflicts occur not only between avowed enemies, but between family members and close friends. Our inborn selfishness provides countless opportunities to clash with others who are also naturally selfish. These conflicts can be multi-faceted and complex. They may be fueled by sinister things like hatred and pride or by innocent things like misunderstandings and personality differences.[1]

When we are in the middle of a conflict, it is always import-  ant to analyze ourselves first. What are we doing that others find offensive? Why are we behaving the way we are? Are there root issues of pride and insecurity in our own lives that we need to address? How have we made the conflict worse? What could we do to make it better?

We can solve many problems by approaching a conflict with the desire to solve it, rather than merely to blame it on the other party. This will usually involve open communication. We will allow those on the other side to explain themselves without interruption, and we will try to see

1   John Coblentz, *Getting Along with People God's Way* (Harrisonburg, VA: Christian Light Publications, Inc., 2008), pp. 123, 128, 132.

the situation from their point of view. We will be willing to say things like, "I was wrong. I'm sorry. Please forgive me."

Still, there will be times when we face conflicts we did not instigate and that we are powerless to solve. The old adage, "It takes two to fight," doesn't address what happens when one person is fighting and the other is not. People do misuse and abuse others who are innocent. Sometimes those who seem least deserving of harsh, unfair treatment receive the most. Yet even when we suffer unjustly, it is possible to be faithful to the commands of God and the law of love.

In the rest of this booklet, we will focus on the difficulties innocent people face. How are they mistreated? What motivates abusive behavior? How does a follower of Christ respond? Can anything good possibly come from the pain others bring into our lives?

7

WAYS OTHERS MAKE LIFE DIFFICULT

And others had trial of cruel mockings and scourgings, yea, moreover of bonds and imprisonment: they were stoned, they were sawn asunder, were tempted, were slain with the sword: they wandered about in sheepskins and goatskins; being destitute, afflicted, tormented; (of whom the world was not worthy:) they wandered in deserts, and in mountains, and in dens and caves of the earth.
—Hebrews 11:36–38

Less than three hundred years after Jesus' death and resurrection, a young man named Maximilian from the north African nation of Numidia heard the Gospel and responded to its message. He read Jesus' words about love and forgiveness, and he determined to follow the teachings of his Lord.

Maximilian was only 21 years old when he was recruited to join the Roman army. Standing bravely before the proconsul, Maximilian refused to join the army. "I cannot do it because I am a Christian," he explained.

When the proconsul countered that other Christians had served in the army, Maximilian replied, "They know what is fitting for them, but I know what Christ wants me to do." Seeing that persuasion would not change Maximilian's mind, the proconsul pronounced his sentence. At twenty-one years old, Maximilian was beheaded for his loyalty to Christ's commands.[1]

Since the time sin entered this world, innocent people have suffered at the hands of others. Cataloging the ways they have suffered would fill volumes. The Biblical record itself could be called *The Book of Suffering*. Abel was murdered because of his brother's envy. Abraham received inferior land as a result of his nephew's selfishness. The greed of his enemy cost Isaac the wells he had dug. Joseph was sold into slavery at the hands of his

---

1 Elizabeth Hershberger Bauman, *Coals of Fire* (Scottdale, PA: Herald Press, 1994), p. 29.

jealous brothers. We could add many more examples without leaving the book of Genesis! People hurting people is a universal theme of history.

The types of suffering people inflict on others can be roughly divided into two categories—psychological and physical. Often, abusive behavior contains elements of both. As we prepare to move on in our study, it is helpful to think a bit more about the specific ways innocent people suffer. Consider the lists below.

Psychological abuse attempts to destroy a person's morale. It may include, but is not limited to:

- **Ridicule:** "What are you thinking? How could you possibly do it that way?"
- **Slander:** "You are the most ignorant person I know."
- **Intimidation:** "If you do _____, I'm going to _____."
- **Criticism:** "Why can't you ever do

anything right?"[2]

- **Rejection:** "No, I really don't think you'd be welcome at the party."
- **Mocking:** "Hey, everybody, watch how _____ plays volleyball. He can't even hit it!"
- **Blame:** "It's all your fault. If it wasn't for you, this never would have happened!"
- **False accusations:** accusing others of things known to be untrue
- **Avoidance:** avoiding eye contact, conversation, and interaction of any kind

For the sake of this discussion, I use the term _physical abuse_ to mean anything that moves beyond the verbal, non-tangible realm. Here are some examples:

- **Stalking:** unwanted attention, phone calls, emails, threats
- **Destruction of property:** graffiti, vandalism
- **Riots:** uncontrolled mobs, irrational demands, firebombs
- **Identity fraud:** assuming the identity of another for financial gain

---

2 Simon Schrock, _Don't Throw in the Towel_ (Harrisonburg, VA: Vision Publishers, 2003), p.48.

- **Sexual abuse:** abuse of another for one's own sexual gratification
- **Theft:** taking what belongs to another without the owner's consent
- **Unjust imprisonment:** imprisoning the innocent
- **Bodily harm:** stoning, beating, amputation, burning
- **Murder:** the taking of life

Sometimes mistreatment feels random, completely without cause; but is it really? Do innocent people ever suffer at the hands of others for absolutely no reason? Why do people make our lives difficult, anyway?

8

WHY OTHERS MAKE LIFE DIFFICULT

When Sanballat the Horonite, and Tobiah the servant, the Ammonite, heard of it, it grieved them exceedingly that there was come a man to seek the welfare of the children of Israel. . . . Now Tobiah the Ammonite was by him, and he said, Even that which they build, if a fox go up, he shall even break down their stone wall.
—Nehemiah 2:10; 4:3

The story of Nehemiah is a fascinating account of innocent people facing unwarranted opposition. And it is a window into some of the reasons why ordinary people face some extraordinary problems when dealing with others.

The kinds of opposition Nehemiah and his men received from Sanballat, Tobiah, and crew are typical of the ways people mistreat others. Sanballat and Tobiah resorted to ridicule and false accusations. Not only did they deride the strength of the walls by asserting that a fox could knock them down, but they also accused the Jews of plotting against the king (Nehemiah 2:19; 4:2; 6:2).[1]

What motivated Sanballat and his cronies to treat Nehemiah this way? Looking closely at the story and reading a bit between the lines, we can infer several things.

- **They were afraid**: The return of Nehemiah and his people meant that the existing power structure in the land could be changed. Sanballat and his men feared the loss of their position in the community.
- **They were jealous:** The unity of

1   Simon Schrock, *Don't Throw in the Towel*, p. 28.

Nehemiah and his men, the favor of the king on their mission, and the speed with which they were able to work were tremendous blessings. Observing this combination, the onlookers were jealous.

- **They were prejudiced:** Underlying everything was a prejudice against the Jews as a people. In the first reference to Sanballat and Tobiah, we are told that "it grieved them exceedingly that there was come a man to seek the welfare of the children of Israel" (Nehemiah 2:10).

The ways these men treated Nehemiah and his men masked the real reasons for their animosity. They tried to hide their fear, jealousy, and prejudice with false accusations and ridicule. Throughout history, humans have tried to cover their own inadequacies by torturing others. Abusive behavior is the symptom; internal conflict is the cause.

While it is not always possible to learn why people are mistreating us, seeking to understand the reason will help equip us to respond correctly and to work toward a solution.

The motivations of Nehemiah's enemies—fear, jealousy, and prejudice—are common reasons for malicious behavior. Consider some additional reasons why people are cruel and abusive:

- **Inferiority**: When one's own personal reputation and status become all-important, one often tries to rise by putting others down. The result is slander, false accusation, and all kinds of other bad behaviors.
- **Guilt**: A person's conscience may be pricked with guilt by the lifestyle or teaching of another. Instead of addressing the root of the problem, the guilty person may redirect his internal unrest into hatred toward the person he or she blames for stirring up the feelings of guilt.
- **Greed**: For some people, the desire to be wealthy is an all-consuming obsession. Never mind that their pursuit means plowing others underfoot in the process. Never mind that it means lying and taking what is not rightfully theirs. In their minds, the end justifies the means.
- **Religious beliefs**: Through the centuries, people have been persecuted in the name of religion. While some religions actually do teach the persecution of those who do not adhere to their brand

of faith, religion is often used merely as a cover for bad behavior. Often, religious persecution is excused as an attempt to eradicate false religious beliefs when it is nothing more than a struggle for control. Many people who persecute in the name of religion are more concerned about power than about religion.

- **Politics**: In politics, a person's positions and party affiliation often become one with the person himself. An attack on one's position or party is easily taken as a personal attack and provokes an angry reaction. Sometimes even the refusal to get involved in politics can enrage the diehard political fan. Political loyalty is a frequent source of irrational, abusive behavior.

- **Bitterness**: Bitterness begins when one allows the sorrow of a tragedy or injustice to fester in his mind. Over time, he directs the pain of the experience toward another individual or a group. As the bitterness grows, he begins to think in irrational ways, often targeting people for persecution who have no connection to his original pain. No wonder the writer to the Hebrews said, "Looking diligently lest any man fail of the grace of God; lest any root of bitterness springing up trouble you, and thereby many be defiled" (Hebrews 12:15).

- **Boredom**: Unfortunately, sometimes boredom plays a part in abusive behaviors. "Idleness is the devil's workshop" is more than just a childhood proverb. When minds that have been trained by a godless society have little else to do, they quickly devise hurtful mischief.

- **Past abuse**: People who hurt others have often been hurt themselves. Acting out of their personal traumas, they seem able to relate only in abusive ways.

People may be motivated by several of the things listed above or by other factors entirely. As we try to understand those who are mistreating us, it helps to know about painful experiences that may be driving their actions.

And, besides understanding why people behave as they do, we must grasp something even more important: we are in a war.

9

SPIRITUAL WARFARE

For we wrestle not against flesh and blood, but against principalities, against powers, against the rulers of the darkness of this world, against spiritual wickedness in high places.
—Ephesians 6:12

The tragedy of Job is a classic tale of woe. Overnight, he descended from wealthy statesman to ragged pauper, from respected sage to scorned loner. He exchanged health and ease for misery and disease, and his former friends became his persecutors.

However, the litany of Job's tragedies is not the whole story. Knowing what Job went through is meaningless without knowing the story behind the story. What was it that started this chain of unfortunate events?

We are told that Job's misery began with a conversation in heaven and was perpetrated by the devil but allowed by God. It was Satan himself who damaged Job's health. "So went Satan forth from the presence of the LORD, and smote Job with sore boils from the sole of his foot unto his crown" (Job 2:7).

Often, in the middle of mistreatment, we fail to see the spiritual aspect of the conflict. We do not take into account the unseen warfare driving the circumstances of our lives. Job had the same problem; he struggled to reconcile the goodness of God with the horrors he was experiencing. What Job did not know was that his greatest enemy, the devil, was doing everything in his power to break Job's devotion to God.

The devil still uses the same tactics against us today. Peter says, "Be sober, be vigilant; because your adversary the devil, as a roaring lion, walketh about, seeking whom he may devour . . ." (1 Peter

5:8). Notice how much this sounds like Satan's habits in Job's day: "And the LORD said unto Satan, From whence comest thou? And Satan answered the LORD, and said, From going to and fro in the earth, and from walking up and down in it" (Job 2:2).

The devil is still roaming the earth with the desire to consume everyone he can. His focus is not on those who are deep in sin, because they are already within his grasp. It is the believers, the ones who have set their faces toward heaven, whom he longs to destroy. In that pursuit, he sometimes uses others, motivating his mercenaries to create havoc for the followers of God.[1]

It is important to remember that spiritual life really is warfare. Although it may feel like the enemy is the neighbor next door, the real enemy is the devil himself.

---

1   Simon Schrock, *Don't Throw in the Towel*, p. 28.

10

ACTIONS OF PEACE

*Blessed are the peacemakers: for they shall
be called the children of God.*
—Matthew 5:9

Peter Miller was an educated man who left the Reformed Church to join the community at the Ephrata Cloister around the time of the Revolutionary War. When he did this, a leader in the Reformed Church, Michael Widman, turned against Peter and made his life miserable. Whenever they met, Widman would spit in Peter's face.

In the course of the war, Michael Widman was suspected of treason and ordered to appear before a military court. Upon hearing the news, Peter Miller hurriedly set out for Valley Forge, walking more than fifty miles through snow. He arrived

just after the court had found Widman guilty and had sentenced him to death by hanging. Peter was already acquainted with the presiding officer, General George Washington, and he pleaded earnestly for Widman's life. General Washington listened respectfully to Peter's appeal but in the end told him that he could not release his friend.

Upon hearing the word *friend,* Peter hastily objected. "Friend!" he exclaimed. "He is my worst enemy—my incessant reviler. For a friend I might not importune you; but Widman being, and having been for years, my worst foe, my malignant, persecuting enemy, my religion teaches me 'to pray for those who despitefully use me.'"

According to the story, General Washington was so moved by this selfless appeal that he changed his mind and pardoned Michael Widman.[1, 2]

Peter Miller showed by his actions that he was serious about following the Biblical way of peace. The love he demonstrated toward his enemy mirrored the love of His Master.

The Scriptures are clear that God wants us to pursue peace (Psalm 34:14; 1 Peter 3:11), and peace involves action! While it is tempting to merely avoid those who torment us, this is not God's call. Instead He calls us to act—to confront hatred with love.

The following Scriptures explain just how this is done. Notice the many words that call the believer to action [emphasis mine]:

- "*Love* your enemies, *bless* them that curse you, *do good* to them that hate you, and *pray* for them which despitefully use you, and persecute you . . ." (Matthew 5:44).

- "And if any man will sue thee at the law, and take away thy coat, *let him have* thy cloke also. And whosoever shall compel

1   Dr. John Palo, "The Day Washington Cried," *The Rosicrucian Digest*, August 1962, <http://rosicrucian.50webs.com/various/palo-day-washington-cried.htm>, accessed on March 15, 2012.

2   J.C. Wenger, *The Way of Peace* (Elkhart, IN: Mennonite Board of Missions, 1977), p.38.

thee to go a mile, *go* with him twain. *Give* to him that asketh thee, and from him that would borrow of thee *turn not* thou away" (Matthew 5:40-42).

- "Be not overcome of evil, but *overcome* evil with good" (Romans 12:21).

When we have committed ourselves to Scriptural responses, we will look for ways to love and bless our adversaries. We will intercede for them in prayer. We will do for them what seems unreasonable, giving them what they do not deserve, complying with irrational demands, and extending forgiveness even when it has not been requested.

And we will overcome. We will overcome the evil they plot against us by the good that we do. History brims with the stories of men and women who thwarted the plots of their enemies by heaping good things on them. The guilt and astonishment of their enemies at such unexpected behavior often dissolved their malice.

Actions of peace are not easy. They are not always rewarded in the ways we would hope. Sometimes the rewards come many years in the future. Nonetheless, actions of peace are important for several reasons:

- They follow in the footsteps of the Savior who forgave and blessed His enemies.
- They provide a positive outlet for feelings that could otherwise turn to bitterness.
- They remind us that we have chosen to follow the Scriptural response to evil.
- They help our enemies see that we are serious about our commitment to Christ.
- They show our enemies that we genuinely love and care about them.
- They bring conviction to our enemies.
- They declare plainly to the world that God's kingdom operates on different principles than the kingdom of this world.

Resolve to confront the difficult people in your life with actions of peace.

11

RECIPROCATING MERCY

But God commendeth his love toward us, in that,
while we were yet sinners, Christ died for us.
—Romans 5:8

Many years ago, the only son of a Korean Christian father was murdered by a wicked young man. The judge was about to pronounce his sentence on the murderer when the father of the murdered man asked for permission to speak. The father acknowledged that nothing could be done to bring back his murdered son; and since he no longer had a son, he asked that the judge allow him to adopt the youth who had murdered his son. There was silence in the courtroom at this unusual request, but in the end, the judge granted it, and the story of this father's actions spread throughout Korea.[1]

How could the Korean father do something so radical? How could he look past the evil in the murderer's life and extend love, opportunity, and forgiveness? Had he seen something in the murderer that everyone else failed to see?

I believe the father's secret lay in seeing himself as an unworthy recipient of God's mercy. He knew what it was like to be forgiven, not because of what he had done, but in spite of it. Like the woman who anointed the feet of Jesus, this man loved much because he understood how much he had been forgiven (Luke 7:47). Comprehending the mercy that had been extended to him, he was able to extend the same mercy to another.

We must all live in the light of God's mercy. We may not have murdered, but we have hated. We have broken the law of God, and our just penalty is death. When we were doomed to die, Someone offered to adopt us—to call us children of God (John 1:12). God saw the possibilities in lives that were bruised and broken by sin, and He offered a chance for redemption.

An artist once sat by his studio window and sketched the face of a beggar sitting across the

---

1   J.C. Wenger, p. 6.

street. As the artist worked, he made a few changes to the beggar's likeness. He changed the beggar's eyes from dull and listless to bright and flashing. He stretched the skin on the man's face to give him a look of determination. When he was finished, he called the beggar inside to see the portrait. At first

the beggar did not recognize the face, but then he asked, "Is it me? Can it be me?"

"That's how I see you," said the artist. The beggar stood up straighter. He told the artist that if that is what the artist saw in him, then that was the man he would be.[2]

By seeing the possibilities in a broken life, the artist extended to the beggar a life-changing gift. We have the opportunity to extend similar gifts to others. By extending undeserved love, we follow in the footsteps of Jesus, who gave that kind

2   Simon Schrock, *One Anothering* (Kalona, IA: Calvary Publications, 1986), p. 118.

of love to us. As we do so, we are affirming the efficacy of the power of God—power that can transform anyone!

12

FORGIVENESS

And be ye kind one to another, tenderhearted, forgiving one another, even as God for Christ's sake hath forgiven you.
—Ephesians 4:32

Walking down a street in Jerusalem one day, I watched a young boy reach out and hit another. The boy who had been hit immediately hit back, only his punch was harder than the initial blow. Predictably, the boy who had struck first responded with even more force. This had the makings of an all-out fight.

As I watched the boys returning evil for evil, I thought about how they represented the chronic Israeli-Palestinian conflict. Violence is repaid with more violence; the use of force is avenged with excessive force. Injustices received give license to

mete out greater injustices. Given such predictable reactions, is it any wonder that peace talks have consistently stalled and that progress in resolving the conflict seems hopeless? Since both sides are determined to repay legitimate grievances, how can peace ever be attained?

The solution to the endless spiral of violence in our world is not to respond with more of the same. Pretending that the violence does not exist doesn't help either. Even trying to assess whose violence is the most justified is counterproductive. No, the only solution is to acknowledge the violence, acknowledge the pain and tragedy it has caused, and make a deliberate choice to forgive anyway.

Choosing to forgive is difficult because we are naturally inclined to protect ourselves. When we are affronted, we have to deal with both the pain of the offense and the realization that someone hates us enough to hurt us. Our natural response is to begin building a list of grievances against the offender.

However, forgiveness takes a completely different approach. While we acknowledge wrongdoing, we drop the charges. Such forgiveness is exemplified by the Biblical martyr Stephen, who prayed while being stoned, "Lord, lay not this sin to their charge" (Acts 7:60). He acknowledged his enemies' actions as sin, yet pled with God for mercy. This is forgiveness.[1]

Once we have chosen forgiveness, it becomes a lifestyle. Rather than trying to decide if we can forgive individual offenses, we put on a spirit of forgiveness that looks for opportunities to pardon. Like the father of the Prodigal Son, we live in anticipation of the day when we can extend active forgiveness to the ones our hearts have

---

1   J.C. Wenger, p. 9.

already forgiven.[2]

By choosing to forgive, we acknowledge that nothing can be done to undo the wrongs of the past, so we look instead to the future. We refuse to accept the troubled state of the relationship, but actively work for a brighter tomorrow. While God alone knows how our adversaries will respond, forgiveness lays the foundation for restored relationships and genuine peace.

---

2   Simon Schrock, *One Anothering*, pp. 54, 55.

13

SUFFERING

For unto you it is given in the behalf of
Christ, not only to believe on him, but also
to suffer for his sake . . .
—Philippians 1:29

In 1918, as World War I enveloped America in anti-German sentiment, four German-speaking Hutterite men from South Dakota were drafted for military service. Their belief in the teachings of Jesus, however, would not allow them to participate in war. As a result, the American military officials kept them in solitary confinement in damp, dirty cells. They received little food and had to sleep on wet, cold floors. Two of the men became ill and died. One of the remaining men was released, and one, Jacob Wipf, was detained in prison.

During his imprisonment, Jacob Wipf said, "Sometimes I envy the three who have already been delivered from their pain. Then I think, *Why is the hand of the Lord so heavy upon me? . . . Why must only I continue to suffer?* But then there is joy too, so that I could weep for joy when I think that the Lord considers me worthy to suffer a little for His sake."[1]

Throughout history, the followers of Christ have followed Him through suffering. Christ's response to suffering is an example for all who are called to suffer for His name. "For even hereunto were ye called: because Christ also suffered for us, leaving us an example, that ye should follow his steps: who

1   J.C. Wenger, pp. 53–57.

did no sin, neither was guile found in his mouth: who, when he was reviled, reviled not again; when he suffered, he threatened not; but committed himself to him that judgeth righteously . . ." (1 Peter 2:21–23).

These words were intended for us. While our flesh would love to doubly repay slander or threaten our enemies with revenge, Christ exemplified a different approach. He calls us to commit our suffering to God, allowing Him to mete out vengeance as He chooses.

After all, God is our defender. While we may feel the need to set the record straight, there is tremendous peace in leaving injustices in the hands of God. He is the perfect judge who knows exactly who is right and who is wrong, and He can defend us if He chooses.

When Christ suffered, He looked beyond the suffering to what lay on the other side. As Hebrews 12:2 tells us, ". . . for the joy that was set before him [He] endured the cross, despising the shame, and is set down at the right hand of the throne of God." Suffering believers have the same hope!

14

GOLD FROM THE FIRE

But he knoweth the way that I take: when he hath
tried me, I shall come forth as gold.
—Job 23:10

John Franz was a Mennonite pastor who lived in Montana during World War I. Suspected by his neighbors because of his German roots and hated for his refusal to buy war bonds, John was abducted and almost hung. A group of neighbors, including local law enforcement officers, were the perpetrators of this deed. By the mercy of God, John was spared from the hanging and taken to jail instead. After several days, his church posted bond, and he was released.

Several years passed, and one day a man approached John while he was working. John recognized him as one of the men who had tried to hang him. The man admitted that he had been wrong and asked John to forgive him. Looking at the man, John reached out his hand to him and  said, "I forgive you from my heart."[1] An enemy had become a friend.

In the 1950s, a fierce conflict raged in Kenya between the colonial British government and local Kenyans. National Kenyan believers faced a difficult choice: Would they side with the Kenyans or with the foreigners who ran the government? As church leaders prayed, they came to a decision: they could not fight on either side. They designated a place known as Weithaga as a Christian camp. Anyone could come there as a declaration that they had chosen Jesus' way of peace.

It was not an easy choice. Those who were fighting resented those who refused to fight. Many of the Christians were beaten, and some were killed. But gradually things changed. Some of the people

1   Elizabeth Hershberger Bauman, pp. 31–38.

who had been persecuting the Christians were converted. Their lives drastically changed. The way of peace demonstrated by their Kenyan brothers had brought them to Christ.[2]

Throughout this study, we have looked at the ways innocent people suffer at the hands of others. We have looked at the ways Christians are called to respond. These responses do not always guarantee visible results. There is no promise that our adversary will ask forgiveness as John Franz's enemy did. We are not assured that we will see our persecutors turn to Christ as the Kenyans' neighbors did. Yet we are promised that there will be fruit. We are assured that at the end of our trials, good will come.

Sometimes the gold that emerges from the fires of our suffering comes in the form of personal character development; sometimes it comes in the lives of those who observe our trials; and sometimes it comes in the lives of those who cause our pain. Regardless, we can know that what our enemy means for evil, God can use for good (Genesis 50:20).

So we press on. Even though people malign us and hurt us, even though we despair of the

---

2   J.C. Wenger, pp. 39–41.

difficult people who badger us, we remember. We remember who God is. We remember who we are. We remember that the hurts we receive at the hands of others may be tools God will use to create beauty in our lives and in our world. And we remember that God can be completely trusted, even when life is difficult.

ABOUT THE AUTHOR

Daniel Miller grew up in the mountains of rural West Virginia, but he has always loved to be with people and is fascinated by human behavior. His ten years as a school teacher gave him many opportunities to observe and ponder the way people interact. The years he spent living in a crowded, conflict-ridden area of the Middle East also provided insightful glimpses into human relationships. Currently, Daniel lives in Harrisonburg, Virginia, with his wife Joetta and their son Malachi.

If you wish to contact Daniel, you may email him at savedfromlions@gmail.com or write to him in care of Christian Aid Ministries, P.O. Box 360, Berlin, Ohio 44610.

CHRISTIAN AID MINISTRIES

Christian Aid Ministries was founded in 1981 as a nonprofit, tax-exempt 501(c)(3) organization. Its primary purpose is to provide a trustworthy and efficient channel for Amish, Mennonite, and other conservative Anabaptist groups and individuals to minister to physical and spiritual needs around the world. This is in response to the command ". . . do good unto all men, especially unto them who are of the household of faith" (Galatians 6:10).

Each year, CAM supporters provide approximately 15 million pounds of food, clothing, medicines, seeds, Bibles, Bible story books, and other Christian literature for needy people. Most of the aid goes to orphans and Christian families. Supporters' funds also help clean up and rebuild for natural disaster victims, put up Gospel billboards in the U.S., support several church-planting efforts, operate two medical clinics, and provide resources for needy families to make their own living. CAM's main purposes for providing aid are to help and encourage God's people and bring the Gospel to a lost and dying world.

CAM has staff, warehouse, and distribution networks in Romania, Moldova, Ukraine, Haiti, Nicaragua, Liberia, and Israel. Aside from management, supervisory personnel, and bookkeeping operations, volunteers do most of the work at CAM locations. Each year, volunteers at our warehouses, field bases, DRS projects, and other locations donate over 200,000 hours of work.

CAM's ultimate purpose is to glorify God and help enlarge His kingdom. ". . . whatsoever ye do, do all to the glory of God" (1 Corinthians 10:31).

THE WAY TO GOD AND PEACE

We live in a world contaminated by sin. Sin is anything that goes against God's holy standards. When we do not follow the guidelines that God our Creator gave us, we are guilty of sin. Sin separates us from God, the source of life.

Since the time when the first man and woman, Adam and Eve, sinned in the Garden of Eden, sin has been universal. The Bible says that we all have "sinned and come short of the glory of God" (Romans 3:23). It also says that the natural consequence for that sin is eternal death, or punishment in an eternal hell: "Then when lust hath conceived, it bringeth forth sin: and sin, when it is finished, bringeth forth death" (James 1:15).

But we do not have to suffer eternal death in hell. God provided forgiveness for our sins through the death of His only Son, Jesus Christ.

Because Jesus was perfect and without sin, He could die in our place. "For God so loved the world that he gave his only begotten Son, that whosoever believeth in him should not perish, but have everlasting life" (John 3:16).

A sacrifice is something given to benefit someone else. It costs the giver greatly. Jesus was God's sacrifice. Jesus' death takes away the penalty of sin for everyone who accepts this sacrifice and truly repents of their sins. To repent of sins means to be truly sorry for and turn away from the things we have done that have violated God's standards (Acts 2:38; 3:19).

Jesus died, but He did not remain dead. After three days, God's Spirit miraculously raised Him to life again. God's Spirit does something similar in us. When we receive Jesus as our sacrifice and repent of our sins, our hearts are changed. We become spiritually alive! We develop new desires and attitudes (2 Corinthians 5:17). We begin to make choices that please God (1 John 3:9). If we do fail and commit sins, we can ask God for forgiveness. "If we confess our sins, he is faithful and just to forgive us our sins, and to cleanse us from all unrighteousness" (1 John 1:9).

Once our hearts have been changed, we want to

continue growing spiritually. We will be happy to let Jesus be the Master of our lives and will want to become more like Him. To do this, we must meditate on God's Word and commune with God in prayer. We will testify to others of this change by being baptized and sharing the good news of God's victory over sin and death. Fellowship with a faithful group of believers will strengthen our walk with God (1 John 1:7).